TEAM SPIRIT®
SMART BOOKS FOR YOUNG FANS

THE LAS VEGAS RAIDERS

BY
MARK STEWART

NorwoodHouse Press

Norwood House Press
2544 Clinton Street
Buffalo, NY 14224

All photos, including cover, courtesy of Getty Images, except: Upper Case Editorial Services (6, 8, 10, 18, 21, 22, 23, 24, 26, 34 right, 35 top left & bottom, 37, 41, 43), Author's Collection (15, 16, 20, 32, 35 top right, 39), Raiders/NFL (17, 36), PRO/NFL Properties (27, 33), Airman Apprentice Raynel Emmons, U.S. Navy (38), Q.B. Inc. (42 right).

The memorabilia, artifacts, and media images that are pictured in this book are presented for educational and informational purposes and come from the collection of the author.

Art Director: Lisa Miley
Series Design: Ron Jaffe
Project Management: Upper Case Editorial Services LLC
Special thanks to Topps, Inc.

Cataloging-in-Publication Data

Names: Stewart, Mark, 1960 July 7-.
Title: The Las Vegas Raiders / Mark Stewart.
Description: Third edition. | Buffalo, NY : Norwood House Press, 2026. | Series: Team spirit | Includes glossary and index.
Identifiers: ISBN 9781978576179 (pbk.) | ISBN 9781978576186 (library bound) | ISBN 9781978576193 (ebook)
Subjects: LCSH: Las Vegas Raiders (Football team)--Juvenile literature. | Las Vegas Raiders (Football team)--History--Juvenile literature. | Oakland Raiders (Football team)--Juvenile literature.
Classification: LCC GV956.L59 S74 2026 | DDC 796.332'6409793135--dc23

CPSIA compliance information: Batch #CSNHP26: For further information contact Norwood House Press at 1-800-237-9932.

Manufactured in the United States of America.

TABLE OF CONTENTS

ABOUT OUR GLOSSARY

In this book, there may be several words that you are reading for the first time. Some are sports words, some are new vocabulary words, and some are familiar words that are used in an unusual way. All of these words are defined on page 46. Throughout the book, sports words appear in **bold type**. Regular vocabulary words appear in ***bold italic type***.

RAIDERS
BOWERS
89

MAKING THE RAIDERS

Most football teams like to copy success. What one team does well, other players and coaches try to do, too. The Las Vegas Raiders are not most football teams. In fact, they take great pride in being different. They like to do things their own way.

To make the Raiders, it helps to have an unusual or extraordinary skill. The team will find a way to make the most of it. The Raiders like to surprise their opponents and ***intimidate*** them, too. Their fans have come to expect the unexpected.

This book tells the story of the Raiders. There is a family feel in the team's locker room, and the players remain close years after they hang up their uniforms. Whether you take the field for the "silver and black" or root for them, you can count on being a Raider for life.

Ameer Abdullah and Brock Bowers celebrate a touchdown during the 2024 season. The Raiders play the game with great joy.

BUILDING BLOCKS

The team that plays its games in pro football's warmest city nearly began in the sport's coldest. In 1960, the **American Football League (AFL)** began plays as a rival to the older **National Football League (NFL)**. The AFL planned to place a team in Minnesota. However, at the last minute, the owners of that club decided they would rather join the NFL. The AFL quickly replaced them with a team in Oakland, California, and called them the Raiders.

The Raiders struggled at first. They won only nine games in their first three seasons. In 1963, Al Davis was hired to coach the team on the field and run its business off the field. He built the Raiders around talented, young players such as Jim Otto, Clem Daniels, Tom Flores, and Fred Williamson. Oakland had a winning record in its first season under Davis.

The Raiders kept adding good players

through smart trades and the **draft**. From 1965 to 1980, Oakland had a winning record every year. During the 1960s, the team's stars included Daryle Lamonica, Fred Biletnikoff, Billy Cannon, Warren Wells, Gene Upshaw, Ben Davidson, Tom Keating, Dan Conners, Dave Grayson, and Willie Brown.

In 1966, the AFL and NFL agreed it would be best to join forces. The merger was set for 1970. A big step in their strategy was starting the **Super Bowl**, which matched the winner of each league for the championship of ***professional*** football. The Raiders won the AFL title in 1967 and played in Super Bowl II. Unfortunately, they lost to the Green Bay Packers.

Oakland's next trip to the Super Bowl came nine years later, under coach John Madden. Quarterback Ken Stabler led the offense. His receivers included Biletnikoff, Dave Casper, and speedy Cliff Branch. Oakland's defense was known as the "Legion of Doom." It starred John Matuszak, Otis Sistrunk, Ted Hendricks, Phil Villapiano, and Jack Tatum. This group led the Raiders to victory against that

LEFT: Al Davis watches the clock tick down on another Oakland victory.
ABOVE: John Madden congratulates Cliff Branch after a touchdown.

RAIDERS
32
MANLEY

team from Minnesota, the Vikings, in Super Bowl XI.

The Raiders won the Super Bowl twice more in the early 1980s. Their coach was Flores, the club's quarterback from the 1960s. Quarterback Jim Plunkett guided the offense. The defense featured Hendricks, Lester Hayes, Rod Martin, Matt Millen, and Howie Long. These teams were rough and tough, and they loved to win.

The Raiders also loved playing for the fans of Oakland. But Davis—who now owned the team—didn't always get along with city officials. In 1982, the Raiders moved to Los Angeles, in the southern part of California. They played there for 13 seasons. Their stars included Marcus Allen, Todd Christensen, Tim Brown, Bo Jackson, Steve Wisniewski, Vann McElroy, and Terry McDaniel. The team also welcomed players who had been stars with other teams, such as Bob Golic, Jay Schroeder, Jeff Hostetler, Willie Gault, Ronnie Lott, and Mike Haynes.

The Raiders returned to Oakland in 1995. They rebuilt their

LEFT: Marcus Allen barrels through three Washington Redskins to pick up a first down.
ABOVE: Fans pack the Raiders' old stadium in Oakland, California.

team and won the West **Division** of the **American Football Conference (AFC)** each season from 2000 to 2002. Quarterback Rich Gannon, kicker Sebastian Janikowski, and defensive star Charles Woodson led this era of success. In January of 2003—after nearly 20 years—the Raiders returned to the Super Bowl. They lost to the Tampa Bay Buccaneers, who shut down Gannon and his teammates with great defense. Tampa Bay's coach, Jon Gruden, had coached the Raiders the year before and knew their playbook from cover to cover. Had Oakland played anyone else, they almost certainly would have won.

In the years that followed, the Raiders struggled to play winning football. Between 2003 and 2019, they made it back to the **playoffs** only once. It was not for lack of talent. Quarterback Derek Carr, receivers Amari Cooper and Marcel Reece, and offensive linemen Kelechi Osemele and Rodney Hudson were among the best players at their position. Linebacker Khalil Mack and cornerback Nnamdi Asomugha were excellent defensive leaders.

During this time, "Raider Nation" received the sad news that Al Davis had passed away. The death of the Raiders' longtime leader during the 2011 season marked the end of an amazing chapter in football history and began a new one that would lead the team to move for a fourth time. In 2020, the Raiders left Oakland and moved to Las Vegas, Nevada. In just their second year there, the team went 10–7 and returned to the playoffs. Carr threw for 27 touchdowns and nearly 5,000 yards. The team's new stars included running back Josh Jacobs, receivers Hunter Renfroe and Darren Waller, and punter A.J. Cole III. The defense was led by lineman Maxx Crosby, who specialized in crashing into the backfield to break up running and passing plays.

The move to Las Vegas surprised many old-time fans. The city is a favorite ***destination*** for people who enjoy gambling—which includes betting on sports. The NFL has always had very strict rules against betting for the people who work and play for its teams. But over the years, the league also has seen that betting has increased interest in pro football. The Raiders have not only enjoyed their new home, they have made new fans of people who visit Las Vegas from all over the world.

LEFT: Charles Woodson **ABOVE**: Raiders fans are loud, proud—and different.

LAS VEGAS
RAIDER
50
CROSBY
McCAFFREY
KITTLE

GAME DAY

The Raiders have hosted their games in four cities. During their first six seasons, they played in and around San Francisco. In 1966, the Raiders moved into a new home, Oakland-Alameda County Stadium. They stayed there until 1982, when they moved again, this time to Los Angeles. The team played there for more than a ***decade***. The Raiders moved back to Oakland for the 1995 season. In 2020, they left California for the neighboring state of Nevada and became the Las Vegas Raiders.

Temperatures in Las Vegas often reach 90 degrees Fahrenheit (32 degrees Celsius) or more, even during football season. The Raiders' new stadium has a dome to keep the players and fans cool on hot days. The field is also home to the University of Nevada, Las Vegas (UNLV) Rebels.

BY THE NUMBERS

- *The stadium cost $1.9 billion, making it one of the most expensive in the world.*
- *The Raiders' stadium has 65,000 seats for football.*
- *In 2028, the college basketball Final Four and National Championship game is scheduled for the stadium. More than 5,000 field-level seats will be added for the games.*

The team's new stadium features a domed roof to keep fans comfortable.

RAIDERS
98
98

TEAM COLORS

The Raiders have worn their famous silver and black uniforms since 1963. But Oakland's first colors were black and gold. The team used black helmets with a white stripe and no ***logo***. Al Davis replaced them with a silver helmet with a black stripe.

Davis also added the team logo to the helmet. It showed a pirate wearing a football helmet, along with a shield and two crossed swords. The logo has become one of the best known in sports.

Today, the Raiders wear uniforms that are almost identical to their style from the 1960s. They usually play in black jerseys for home games. Occasionally, the Raiders wear white at home. They did that for the first time in 2008 to cool down when the temperature on the field soared above 90 degrees Fahrenheit (32 degrees Celsius).

LEFT: Maxx Crosby shows off the Raiders' famous silver-and-black uniform.
ABOVE: Oakland fans wore this patch on their jackets in the 1970s.

LAST TEAM STANDING

The Raiders were one of the most successful teams in pro football during the 1960s. From 1967 to 1969, they lost just four games in three seasons. Oakland captured its first title in 1967 when it won the AFL championship. The team played in the second-ever Super Bowl against the Green Bay Packers and lost. Nine years later, the Raiders returned to the Super Bowl and this time they won.

Oakland went 13–1 in the regular season and then won a thrilling playoff game against the New England Patriots. Trailing in the fourth quarter, Ken Stabler led two late touchdown drives to produce a 24–21 victory. Next, Oakland beat the Pittsburgh Steelers in the AFC title game to earn a trip to Super Bowl XI.

The Raiders went into the Super Bowl feeling that they couldn't lose. The Minnesota Vikings were helpless against the powerful

LEFT: Fans bought this program at Super Bowl II.
RIGHT: Kenny King

Oakland defense. The Raiders led 16–0 after two quarters and continued to roll in the second half. Moments after Pete Banaszak ran for his second touchdown of the game, Willie Brown intercepted a pass and went 75 yards for another score. The Raiders won easily, 32–14.

Oakland's next championship came against the Philadelphia Eagles in Super Bowl XV. The Raiders made the playoffs with a team full of ***castoffs*** from other clubs. Quarterback Jim Plunkett, running back Kenny King, and defensive end John Matuszak were signed by Al Davis after their old teams had given up on them.

Against the Eagles, the Raiders were unstoppable. Plunkett threw two touchdown passes in the first quarter. The first went to Cliff Branch. The second was an 80-yard strike to King. Meanwhile, the Oakland defense was ***dominant***. Matt Millen made plays all over the field, and Rod Martin intercepted three passes. The Raiders cruised to a 27–10 victory.

Three years later, the Raiders—now playing in Los Angeles—

faced the Washington Redskins (now the Commanders) in Super Bowl XVIII. Plunkett was still the quarterback, but new young stars led the team. Marcus Allen ran for more than 1,000 yards and tight end Todd Christensen caught more than 90 passes during the 1983 season. The defense starred Millen, Howie Long, and Lester Hayes.

The Redskins were the defending Super Bowl champions. Earlier in the year, they had defeated the Raiders in an exciting contest, 37–35. In the first half of their rematch, John Riggins could find no running room against the Los Angeles defense. When the Redskins tried to pass, Hayes and Mike Haynes blanketed the Washington receivers.

The Raiders held a 14–3 lead just before halftime. With 12 seconds left, Washington tried a short pass. Linebacker Jack

Squirek plucked it out of the air and ran the interception back for a touchdown. Oakland poured it on in the second half. The play that broke the game open was a 74-yard run by Allen. The Raiders won their third NFL championship, 38–9. Allen set a Super Bowl record with 191 rushing yards.

LEFT: Jim Plunkett spots an open receiver. **ABOVE**: Marcus Allen breaks into the clear on his 74-yard touchdown run in Super Bowl XVIII.

LEADING LIGHTS

Some players lead with their words. Others lead with their actions. The greatest Raiders inspired their teammates and thrilled their fans by doing both. They are the team's brightest stars…

JIM OTTO — Offensive Lineman

• Born: 1/5/1938 • Died: 5/19/2024

• Played for Team: 1960 to 1974

Jim Otto did not miss a game during his entire career in Oakland. That was amazing since most teams thought he was too small to play pro football. Otto signed with the Raiders, built up his body, and played center for 15 seasons.

FRED BILETNIKOFF — Receiver

• Born: 2/23/1943 • Played for Team: 1965 to 1978

"Too small, too slow"—that is what the scouts said about Fred Biletnikoff when he began his career in the AFL. They left out "too smart." Biletnikoff caught 40 or more passes 10 years in a row. He finished his career with 589 receptions.

ABOVE: Jim Otto **RIGHT**: Gene Upshaw talks strategy with Daryle Lamonica.

GENE UPSHAW — Offensive Lineman

• BORN: 8/15/1945 • DIED: 8/20/2008
• PLAYED FOR TEAM: 1967 TO 1981

Gene Upshaw was fast and powerful. Once Upshaw latched onto a defender, he usually knocked him flat on his back. Upshaw was also a great leader.

DARYLE LAMONICA — Quarterback

• BORN: 7/17/1941 • DIED: 4/21/2022 • PLAYED FOR TEAM: 1967 TO 1974

Daryle Lamonica was known as the "Mad Bomber" because no one threw long passes better than he did. Lamonica joined the Raiders after spending four years on the bench with the Buffalo Bills. He led the league in touchdown passes in 1967 and 1969—and was an **All-Pro** in both those seasons, too.

GEORGE BLANDA — Kicker/Quarterback

• BORN: 9/17/1927 • DIED: 9/27/2010 • PLAYED FOR TEAM: 1967 TO 1975

George Blanda was one of the most reliable players in team history. His clutch field goals helped Oakland win many games. In 1970, Blanda passed the Raiders to the AFC title game. He retired with the pro football record of 2,002 points.

WILLIE BROWN — Defensive Back

• BORN: 12/2/1940 • DIED: 10/22/2019 • PLAYED FOR TEAM: 1967 TO 1978

Willie Brown was a master at one-on-one coverage. He was strong and quick, so he could stay close to any receiver. Brown was an All-Pro four times for the Raiders. In Super Bowl XI, he intercepted a pass and returned it 75 yards for a touchdown.

ART SHELL — Offensive Lineman

• BORN: 11/26/1946 • PLAYED FOR TEAM: 1968 TO 1982

Art Shell was big, fast, and smart. When the Oakland offense needed to open a hole, it looked to him and teammate Gene Upshaw. Later Shell became the first African American head coach in the NFL's **modern era.**

KEN STABLER — Quarterback

• BORN: 12/25/1945 • DIED: 7/8/2015 • PLAYED FOR TEAM: 1968 TO 1979

Ken Stabler was an accurate passer who had a knack for wriggling out of tight spots. The "Snake" guided Oakland to its first Super Bowl victory. He was voted the NFL Most Valuable Player (MVP) in 1974.

PHIL VILLAPIANO — Linebacker

• BORN: 2/26/1949 • PLAYED FOR TEAM: 1971 TO 1979

No one brought more energy to a football field than Phil Villapiano. He was one of the fastest, hardest-hitting linebackers in the league. Villapiano's goal-line tackle against the Vikings in Super Bowl XI turned the game around and helped the Raiders win their first championship.

CLIFF BRANCH — Receiver

• BORN: 8/1/1948 • DIED: 8/3/2019 • PLAYED FOR TEAM: 1972 TO 1985

When the Raiders needed a first down, they threw the ball to Fred Biletnikoff or Dave Casper. When they needed a touchdown, Cliff Branch was their man.

ABOVE: Ken Stabler **RIGHT**: Tim Brown goes out for a pass.

RAY GUY

Punter

• Born: 12/22/1949 • Died: 11/3/2022 • Played for Team: 1973 to 1986

Ray Guy spent his entire 14-year career with the Raiders. Many experts believe he is the greatest punter in NFL history. Guy's right leg was like a cannon. He regularly boomed punts more than 60 yards. Guy's career average was 42.2 yards per punt.

HOWIE LONG

Defensive Lineman

• Born: 1/6/1960 • Played for Team: 1981 to 1993

Teams that played the Raiders in the 1980s usually double-teamed Howie Long. Even so, Long was still able to make plays. He had the speed to chase down running backs or sack the quarterback.

MARCUS ALLEN

Running Back

• Born: 3/26/1960 • Played for Team: 1982 to 1992

Marcus Allen was a smooth and powerful runner. Each season from 1983 to 1985, he ran for at least 1,000 yards and caught more than 60 passes. Allen was the MVP of Super Bowl XVIII and also the NFL MVP in 1985.

TIM BROWN

Receiver

• Born: 7/22/1966 • Played for Team: 1988 to 2003

Tim Brown spent 16 years catching passes for the Raiders. Brown hauled in more than 1,000 in all. He could do it all, and often did. In 1994, Brown led the AFC in pass receptions and punt returns. By the time he left the game, everyone called him "Mr. Raider."

RICH GANNON — Quarterback

• BORN: 12/20/1965 • PLAYED FOR TEAM: 1999 TO 2004

Rich Gannon struggled through 11 NFL seasons before the Raiders signed him and made him their starting quarterback. Gannon became a great team leader. He was the league MVP in 2002 when he guided Oakland to Super Bowl XXXVII.

CHARLES WOODSON — Defensive Back

• BORN: 10/7/1976 • PLAYED FOR TEAM: 1998 TO 2005

Charles Woodson was a standout from his very first game for the Raiders. In 1998, he was voted Defensive **Rookie** of the Year. Woodson was named to the **Pro Bowl** in each of his first four seasons in Oakland. He had 17 interceptions during his career with the team.

SEBASTIAN JANIKOWSKI — Kicker

• BORN: 3/2/1978 • PLAYED FOR TEAM: 2000 TO 2016

The Raiders have a proud history of great kickers. Sebastian Janikowski may have been the best of all of them. He had a very strong leg and regularly made field goals of more than 50 yards.

DEREK CARR — Quarterback

• BORN: 3/28/1991 • PLAYED FOR TEAM: 2014 TO 2022

Derek Carr threw for more than 4,000 yards four times and finished third in the MVP voting in 2016. He was a Pro Bowl pick four times with the Raiders and finished as the team's all-time passing leader with more than 35,000 yards.

JOSH JACOBS

Running Back

• Born: 2/11/1998 • Played for Team: 2019 to 2023

In five years with the Raiders, Josh Jacobs ran for more than 1,000 yards three times and was the NFL rushing leader in 2002 with 1,653 yards. He showed great skill in waiting for his blockers to open a hole and then powering through it. Jacobs was hardly the fastest runner in the NFL, but he was definitely one of the toughest to tackle.

MAXX CROSBY

Defensive Lineman

• Born: 8/22/1997 • First Season with Team: 2019

One of the keys to a good draft is waiting as long as possible to grab a player you love. In 2019, the Raiders were able to get Maxx Crosby in the fourth round and he was named Defensive Player of the Week less than three months into his rookie season. In 2023, Crosby made the 50th sack of his career and was honored as an All-Pro for the second time.

BROCK BOWERS

Tight End

• Born: 12/13/2002 • First Season with Team: 2024

Brock Bowers was an **All-American** three times in college and was the Raiders' top draft pick in 2024. Las Vegas fans fell in love with his pass-catching and blocking skills during his first season. He had 112 receptions to set a new record for NFL for rookies.

LEFT: Rich Gannon

X'S & O'S

Al Davis was the Oakland coach for just three seasons, but no one had a bigger impact on the team. Davis was successful for many reasons. He created a special togetherness among the players and made them feel like they were part of his family. Davis was also good at finding stars who were overlooked by other teams. In Oakland, they got a warm welcome from teammates and fans.

After he became the team owner, Davis developed a good eye for coaches, too. John Rauch, John Madden, and Tom Flores each led the team to a Super Bowl under him. Rauch was hired to coach the Raiders in 1966, after Davis agreed to become ***commissioner*** of the AFL. In his second season, Rauch guided Oakland to the league title. But Davis could not resist "helping" Rauch with even the tiniest decisions. So in 1969, Rauch left to coach the Buffalo Bills.

From then on, Davis made it clear to his coaches that they could expect to hear his opinions on a regular basis. That didn't bother

Madden. He was promoted to head coach after Rauch left. Madden won 103 games in 10 seasons. Few people loved football the way he did. Under Madden, the Raiders reached the AFC title game five years in a row. They became a truly fearsome team. Madden coached his players to win but also to send a message—no one messes with Oakland!

For Flores, coaching the Raiders was a kind of homecoming. He had been the team's quarterback from 1960 to 1965. Flores was quiet and thoughtful. Sometimes people forgot he was the coach because Davis was in the news so often. But Flores guided the Raiders to victory in the Super Bowl twice—the most of any of the team's coaches.

Flores was the first Latino head coach in the NFL. He led the team from 1979 to 1987. In 1989, the Raiders gave former All-Pro lineman Art Shell the top job. He became the first African American head coach in the NFL. In 1990, Shell led the club to the AFC title game.

LEFT: Al Davis **ABOVE**: Jim Plunkett and Tom Flores appear on a magazine cover together. Plunkett, whose family came from Mexico, and Flores both had Latino roots.

IN THE MOMENT

JANUARY 4, 1981

Teams from California aren't normally used to playing in cold weather, but that's what the Raiders faced against the Browns in Cleveland. In the second round of the playoffs after the 1980 season, the temperature at kickoff was 4 degrees Fahrenheit (–15 degrees Celsius). It was the coldest day for an NFL game since 1967. To make matters worse, the wind was whipping off Lake Erie. The wind made it feel like –37 degrees Fahrenheit (–38 degrees Celsius)!

The Browns scored first after intercepting a pass by Jim Plunkett. The Raiders got a boost when they blocked Don Cockroft's extra point. Oakland came back a few minutes later to take the lead. Plunkett handed off to Mark van Eeghen, who barreled into the end zone.

Cleveland bounced back in the third quarter to regain the lead. In the fourth quarter, Oakland put together a long drive. Van Eeghen crossed the goal line again to make the score 14–12. Cleveland fans were ***frustrated***. The Raiders didn't seem to be bothered by the freezing weather at all.

As time was running out, the Browns marched down the field. With the ball on the 13-yard line, Cleveland faced a tough decision. Instead of sending out Cockroft to try the game-winning field goal, the Browns called a pass play. Brian Sipe faded back and saw Ozzie Newsome open in the end zone, but Mike Davis was waiting to swoop in. The Oakland safety made the interception and saved the game. It was a perfect example of why the Raiders were great—they often were at their best when the conditions were at their worst.

ABOVE: Mike Davis intercepts a pass in front of Ozzie Newsome.

WAIT . . . WHAT?

DID YOU KNOW?

The most famous pass in Raiders history was caught by a ghost. Dave Casper was one of the top receivers in the NFL during the 1970s. Teammates nicknamed him the "Ghost" after the cartoon character Casper the Friendly Ghost. In a 1977 playoff game against the Baltimore Colts, Casper ran a **post pattern** and caught a long pass that helped send the contest into **overtime.** To this day, Raiders fans call this famous play the "Ghost to the Post."

ABOVE: Dave Casper

DID YOU KNOW?

The NFL's biggest *Star Wars* fans was also a Raiders All-Pro. Lester Hayes was football's top defensive back when he played for the Raiders in the 1970s and 1980s. He wasn't just a *Star Wars* fan—he considered himself an actual Jedi Knight! Hayes insisted that if Luke Skywalker played football, he would be a cornerback. Teammate Mike Haynes was a believer. At the Pro Bowl one year, Hayes informed Haynes, "The Force has told me that you will wear silver and black next year." He was right. The NFL awarded Haynes to the Raiders in 1983 after a complicated legal battle over his contract.

DID YOU KNOW?

During the 1970s, the Raiders were the NFL's greatest practical jokers. The players were almost as competitive off the field as they were on the field. Sometimes the tricks they played could be a little mean, but mostly they were all about building team spirit. Phil Villapiano once broke into John Matuszak's home and switched all the furniture from his bedroom and his kitchen. "Tooz" got the last laugh, however. When Villapiano and his teammates visited the home a month later, they were shocked to find Matuszak had not moved anything back. He liked sleeping close to the food.

UNBELIEVABLE!

There isn't much room in pro football for a 40-something quarterback. That's why the Raiders weren't sure what to do with George Blanda in 1970. Blanda had been with the team for three seasons and would soon turn 43. Football was his life. He led the Houston Oilers (now the Tennessee Titans) to the AFL championship in 1960 and 1961. A year later, he was voted league MVP.

Despite his great career, could Blanda really help the Raiders? It didn't seem like he had much to offer. Besides, Oakland already had two talented passers in Daryle Lamonica and Ken Stabler. But coach John Madden played a hunch and decided that Blanda would serve as the Raiders' kicker and backup quarterback. Sure enough, whenever the Oakland offense struggled,

Madden called on the ***veteran*** to give the team a spark.

Starting in October, Blanda came off the bench five weeks in a row. He threw three touchdown passes in a win over the Pittsburgh Steelers. He kicked a 48-yard field goal in a last-second tie with the Kansas City Chiefs. A week later, he tossed a scoring pass to tie the Cleveland Browns and then booted the game-winning field goal. Blanda produced victories in the next two weeks, too.

As it turned out, Oakland needed every one of those wins. They edged the Chiefs by one victory to reach the playoffs. Lamar Hunt, the owner of the Chiefs, couldn't believe it. "This George Blanda is as good as his father—who used to play for Houston," Hunt joked at one point.

Blanda got the last laugh. He went on to win the Bert Bell Award as pro football's Player of the Year.

LEFT: George Blanda signed this photo with the year he entered the Hall of Fame.
ABOVE: The program from Oakland's win over the Steelers features Marvel characters—but Blanda was the real superhero that day!

IT'S ABOUT TIME

In this timeline, each Super Bowl is listed under the year it was played. Remember that the Super Bowl is held early in the year and is actually part of the previous season. For example, Super Bowl XI was played on January 9, 1977, but it was the championship of the 1976 NFL season.

1960
The Raiders play their first AFL season.

1963
Clem Daniels leads the AFL in rushing.

1974
Ray Guy is the NFL's top punter.

1977
The Raiders win their first Super Bowl.

1980
Lester Hayes is named Defensive Player of the Year.

1984
The Raiders win Super Bowl XVIII.

Ray Guy

Lester Hayes

Jerry Rice

Khalil Mack liked to add "Raider Nation" to his autographs.

1997
Tim Brown leads the NFL with 104 receptions.

2002
Jerry Rice makes his 13th Pro Bowl.

2010
Shane Lechler is named first-team All-Pro for the sixth time.

2016
Khalil Mack is named NFL Defensive Player of the Year.

2020
The Raiders play their first season in Las Vegas.

2024
Brock Bowers is named first-team All-Pro as a rookie.

Shane Lechler

THAT'S A FACT

CITY GUY

Matt Millen was the first player to win the Super Bowl for four different cities. The All-Pro linebacker won two with the Raiders— one in Los Angeles and one in Oakland—and later captured titles with the San Francisco 49ers and Washington Redskins.

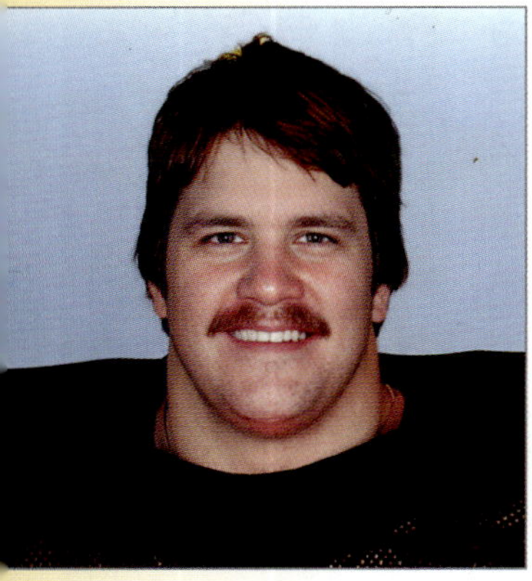

SEA OF HANDS

In 1974, the Miami Dolphins hoped to reach the Super Bowl for a fourth year in a row. The Raiders beat them 28–26 in the playoffs on a touchdown with 24 seconds left in the game. Clarence Davis caught a desperate pass in the middle of three Miami defenders. The play went down in history as the "Sea of Hands."

SIZE DOUBLE-X

Maxx Crosby has an extra X at the end of his first name because he was a huge baby. He was more than 11 ½ pounds (5.2 kg) at birth. XX is the next size up from XL.

HONOR GUARD

After retiring from the Raiders, All-Pro guard Gene Upshaw became the head of the NFL **Players Association**. After he died in 2008, the Raiders added the initials *GU* to their helmets in honor of him.

IT'S A GUY THING

Ray Guy had a leg like a ***bazooka***. During the 1976 Pro Bowl, he punted a ball that hit the video screen hanging above the field in the Louisiana Superdome. Guy was voted the NFL's best all-time punter when the league picked its 75th Anniversary team in 1994.

RUNNING MAN

After receiver Willie Gault retired from the Raiders in 1993, he went back to his first love, track and field. Gault had been one of the fastest men in the world before his NFL career. In 2011, Gault was crowned the over-50 world champion in the 100 meters.

LEFT: Matt Millen
ABOVE: The letters GU can be seen on Darren McFadden's helmet and jersey.

TALKING FOOTBALL

"The Raiders were a team ***steeped*** in history. From the moment I walked into the Raider camp I could feel it."

► **HOWIE LONG,** *on his first season with the Raiders*

"It has been an honor to wear the Silver and Black."

► **FRED BILETNIKOFF,** *on his career with the Raiders*

"By the time I finished playing, I was too old to be starting out as a coach!"

► **GEORGE BLANDA,** *on why he did not have a second career in football*

ABOVE: Howie Long **RIGHT**: Phil Villapiano

"I remember them carrying me off ... and I remember them dropping me."

▶ **JOHN MADDEN,** *on the short victory ride his players gave him after Super Bowl XI*

"The players on that 1976 team were very close. If you asked me to pick a guy on that club who 'didn't belong' it would be very difficult."

▶ **PHIL VILLAPIANO,** *on the closeness of Oakland's championship team*

"I was meant to be a Raider…I don't fit in."

▶ **MAXX CROSBY,** *on what makes him a perfect fit for the team*

"Once a Raider, always a Raider."

▶ **AL DAVIS,** *on his belief that his players were Raiders for life*

ROAD TRIP

For fans of the Raiders, all roads lead to Las Vegas. But each journey begins somewhere else. Match the pushpins on these maps to the Team Facts, and you will discover the ultimate Raiders road trip!

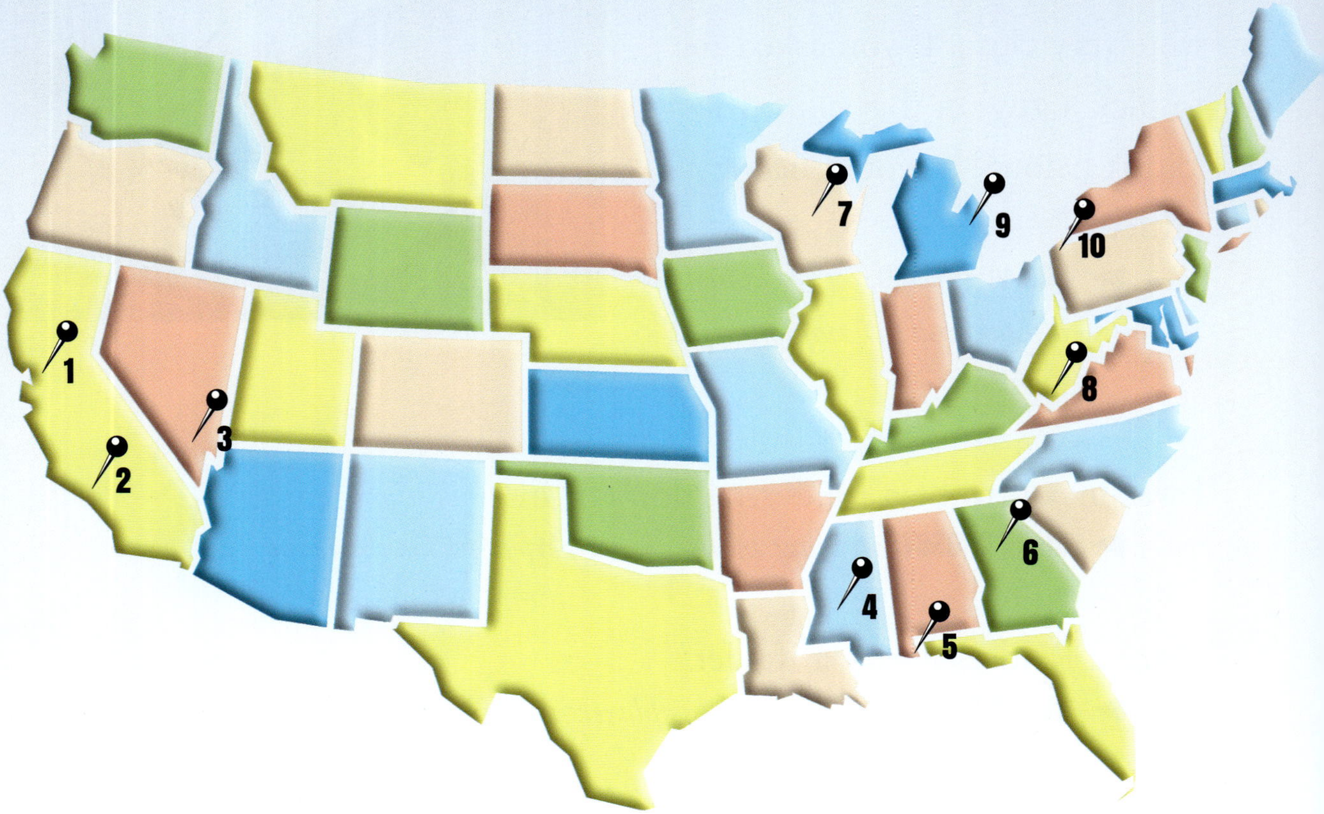

TEAM FACTS

1. **OAKLAND, CALIFORNIA**—The Raiders played here starting in 1960.
2. **LOS ANGELES, CALIFORNIA**—The Raiders played here from 1982 to 1994.
3. **LAS VEGAS, NEVADA**—The Raiders moved here in 2020.
4. **YAZOO CITY, MISSISSIPPI**—Willie Brown was born here.
5. **FOLEY, ALABAMA**—Ken Stabler was born here.
6. **GRIFFIN, GEORGIA**—Willie Gault was born here.
7. **WAUSAU, WISCONSIN**—Jim Otto was born here.
8. **WELCH, WEST VIRGINIA**—Rod Martin was born here.
9. **LAPEER, MICHIGAN**—Maxx Crosby was born here.
10. **ERIE, PENNSYLVANIA**—Fred Biletnikoff was born here
11. **WALBRZYCH, POLAND**—Sebastian Janikowski was born here.
12. **GUATEMALA CITY, GUATEMALA**—Ted Hendricks was born here.
13. **MEXICO CITY, MEXICO**—The Raiders defeated the Houston Texans here in 2016.

Willie Gault

HONOR ROLL

The great Raiders teams and players have left their marks on the record books. These are the best of the best!

ABOVE: Matt Millen celebrates the team's Super Bowl XV win.

RAIDERS ACHIEVEMENTS

ACHIEVEMENT	SEASON
AFL West Champions	1967
AFL Champions*	1967
AFC Champions	1976
Super Bowl XI Champions	1976
AFC Champions	1980
Super Bowl XV Champions	1980
AFC Champions	1983
Super Bowl XVIII Champions	1983
AFC Champions	2002

**Lost Super Bowl II*

RIGHT: Super Bowl QBs Daryle Lamonica, Ken Stabler, George Blanda, and Jim Plunkett pose for a publicity photo.

RAIDERS AWARD WINNERS

WINNER	AWARD	SEASON
Al Davis	AFL Coach of the Year	1963
Archie Matsos	AFL All-Star Game Defensive MVP	1964
Daryle Lamonica	AFL MVP	1967
John Rauch	AFL Coach of the Year	1967
George Atkinson	AFL Defensive Rookie of the Year	1968
Daryle Lamonica	AFL MVP	1969
Ken Stabler	NFL Offensive Player of the Year	1974
Ken Stabler	NFL MVP	1974
Fred Biletnikoff	Super Bowl MVP	1976
Lester Hayes	Defensive Player of the Year	1980
Jim Plunkett	Super Bowl MVP	1980
Marcus Allen	Offensive Rookie of the Year	1982
Marcus Allen	Super Bowl MVP	1983
Marcus Allen	Offensive Player of the Year	1985
Marcus Allen	NFL MVP	1985
Charles Woodson	Defensive Rookie of the Year	1998
Rich Gannon	Pro Bowl Offensive MVP	2001
Rich Gannon	NFL MVP	2002
Rich Gannon	Pro Bowl Offensive MVP	2002
Khalil Mack	Defensive Player of the Year	2016
Maxx Crosby	Pro Bowl Defensive MVP	2022

Rich Gannon

PAYDIRT!

Whenever the Raiders have the football, their fans root for them to "hit paydirt." The saying dates back more than 100 years to the old prospecting days. It is the layer of earth that contains the first bits of gold. In the NFL, touchdowns are the name of the game. Paydirt is the reward for digging deep and doing the hard work it takes to cross the goal line.

During the 1960s, the American Football League was known for its exciting, wide-open playing style. No quarterback captured that style like Daryle Lamonica. He had one of the strongest throwing arms in history and threw to some of the AFL's swiftest receivers. Lamonica might try a 50-yard pass at any time. That was how he got his nickname, the "Mad Bomber." In 1967, Lamonica set a team record with 30 touchdown passes. Two years later, in 1969, he threw for 34. The next time a Raider even came close was in 2015, when Derek Carr threw for 32 scores in 16 games. Lamonica set his record during a 14-game season.

In 1963, Art Powell set a team record when he grabbed 16 scoring passes. That number is remarkable for two reasons. First, it came in a year when the Raiders did not have a star quarterback. Second, Powell's record has never been broken. The Raiders had some sensational receivers in the 1960s and 1970s, including Warren Wells, Cliff Branch, Fred Biletnikoff, Billy Cannon, and Dave Casper. Each of them had a chance to break Powell's record, but none of them did. In recent years, only Davante Adams came close. He caught 14 touchdown passes in 2022.

The team record for rushing touchdowns also dates back to the team's early days. In their first 15 seasons, no Raider running back had even scored 10 touchdowns in a season. In 1975, Pete Banaszak crashed into the end zone 16 times. He had always been good at getting tough yards, so coach John Madden called Banaszak's number whenever the team got close to the goal line.

ABOVE: Pete Banaszak powers through the defense in Super Bowl XI.

GLOSSARY

FOOTBALL WORDS
VOCABULARY WORDS

FOOTBALL WORDS

- **ALL-AMERICAN**—Recognized as being one of the top college players.
- **ALL-PRO**—An honor given to the best players at each position. A "first-team" All-Pro is the best of the best.
- **AMERICAN FOOTBALL CONFERENCE (AFC)**—One of two groups of teams that make up the NFL.
- **AMERICAN FOOTBALL LEAGUE (AFL)**—A league that played from 1960 to 1969 before joining forces with the NFL in 1970.
- **DIVISION**—One of a groups of teams that make up a football conference. The Raiders have played in the AFC West since joining the NFL.
- **DRAFT**—The annual event during which teams pick from the best college players.
- **MODERN ERA**—A period beginning in 1932, when the NFL started holding an official championship game.
- **NATIONAL FOOTBALL LEAGUE (NFL)**—The league that began in 1920 and is still playing today.
- **OVERTIME**—A special period played when the score is tied at the end of 60 minutes.
- **PLAYERS ASSOCIATION**—The union that protects the interests of players.
- **PLAYOFFS**—The series of games after the regular season that lead to the championship game.
- **POST PATTERN**—A pass play where a receiver angles toward the middle of the field.
- **PRO BOWL**—The NFL's all-star game.
- **ROOKIE**—A player in his first professional season.
- **SUPER BOWL**—The annual championship game of pro football. The first Super Bowl was played following the 1966 season.

VOCABULARY WORDS

- *BAZOOKA*—A military weapon that fires an explosive shell.
- *CASTOFFS*—Players who are let go by other teams.
- *COMMISSIONER*—The head of a sports league.
- *DECADE*—A period of ten years.
- *DESTINATION*—A place that people make a special trip to visit.
- *DOMINANT*—Controlling and powerful.
- *FRUSTRATED*—Annoyed because of an inability to achieve something.
- *INTIMIDATE*—Frighten someone into doing what you want.
- *LOGO*—A design or symbol used by a business.
- *PROFESSIONAL*—Done as a paying job.
- *STEEPED*—Filled with a certain quality.
- *VETERAN*—Someone with a lot of experience.

ABOUT THE AUTHOR

MARK STEWART written more than 75 books for kids on pro and college football. He grew up in New York City rooting for the Giants and Jets, and was lucky enough to meet players from both teams. Mark comes from a publishing family. His parents edited and wrote for national magazines and his grandfather was Sunday Editor of *The New York Times*. After graduating with a degree in history from Duke University, Mark wrote for sports and lifestyle magazines and published his first book in 1992. Since then, he has profiled more than 1,000 athletes, many of whom were Raiders—including Marcus Allen, Fred Biletnikoff, George Blanda, Ted Hendricks, Jim Otto, Ken Stabler, Jack Tatum, Art Thoms, and Phil Villapiano, with whom he enjoyed a long friendship.

ON THE ROAD

LAS VEGAS RAIDERS

3333 Al Davis Way
Las Vegas, NV 89118

THE PRO FOOTBALL HALL OF FAME

2121 George Halas Dr.
NW Canton, Ohio 44708
www.profootballhof.com

ON THE BOOKSHELF

To learn more about the sport of football, look for these books at your library or bookstore:

- Berglund, Bruce. *Football GOATs: The Greatest Athletes of All Time*. North Mankato, MN: Capstone Publishing/ Sports Illustrated for Kids, 2022.
- Von Kuczkowski, Alex. *Football: The Ultimate Book.* Dusseldorf, Germany: teNeues Verlag GmbH, 2025.
- Zweig, Eric. *It's A Numbers Game: Football.* Washington, DC: National Geographic Kids, 2022.

INDEX

PAGE NUMBERS IN **BOLD** REFER TO ILLUSTRATIONS.